a primer for movement description using effort-shape

and supplementary concepts · by

cecily dell· **revised edition**

NEW YORK  DANCE NOTATION BUREAU PRESS

1977

Second Edition, June, 1977
Second Printing, October, 1989
Third Printing, October, 1991
Fourth Printing, August 1993

Library of Congress Catalog Card Number 78-111086
ISBN 0-932582-03-6

Printed in the United States of America

Dance Notation Bureau, Inc.
31 West 21st Street
New York, NY 10010

TABLE OF CONTENTS

ACKNOWLEDGEMENTS

Thanks to Irmgard Bartenieff, Aileen Crow, Martha Davis, Allison Jablonko, Dr. Judith Kestenberg, Forrestine Paulay and Kayla Zalk for information, suggestion, support; to Marcia Siegel, without whose combination of writing/editing skill and understanding of Effort/Shape this text would be less intelligible; and to Ursula Corning for generous financial support to the Dance Notation Bureau to provide for this publication and others.

PREFACE

This text is intended as a general guide-
line for movement description, according
to the principles of Effort/Shape, along
with some related concepts which are used
by various observers to supplement Effort/
Shape.

Hopefully, the text can serve as a refer-
ence both for beginners and advanced stu-
dents in Effort/Shape, and for people with
many levels of movement experience. The
information ranges from basic, general
ideas in movement analysis to detailed
distinctions within these concepts as well
as differences of terminology and usage in
some cases. Readers will do well to ab-
sorb the basic ideas before dwelling on
details and differences.

I realize only too well that there is no
single, pure approach to these ideas.
Like all theories which are applied in
more than one context, the ideas are modified to become more relevant to each context, and Effort/Shape is presently being
applied in dance training, actor training,
dance therapy, child development, physical

rehabilitation, cross-cultural research and research in psychology. Thus, what is presented here is the framework of ideas from which each specialist selects and which he modifies to suit the needs of his discipline. I have attempted to do as little disservice to each specialized application as is possible in a general presentation of Effort/Shape theory.

Happily, Rudolf Laban's original formulations of Effort were so rich that the concepts can take the pulls and tugs of modification and still remain within a fairly cohesive framework.

Readers should be patient with themselves and with the material as they take it in. It is difficult to believe that movement is really a language than can be understood as specifically as Laban and his colleagues have perceived it. The tendency is immediately to translate it into more familiar terms - emotions or actions or intellectual systems. But as Laban saw so fully, the moving body has its own life, its own experience, function and expression, and it is that life to which these concepts apply.

This is not a text about teaching movement. Probably, movement education can be greatly helped by skilled observation and description, but how and when to evoke what movement experiences in any student involves judgments and skills quite beyond the scope of this text. Nor will this presentation afford an immediate understanding of movement, but rather a way of organizing one's inquiry about it.

Finally, there is no substitute for the experience of these concepts in movement, in the body, and their verbalization here can only hint at their full value in each person's experience.

INTRODUCTION

Someone moves. You want to describe the
movement. What can you say? You could
start by saying what the person did. You
can choose from among the many intransi-
tive verbs in your vocabulary - he ran, he
stooped, he turned, he jumped, he walked,
he sat. Or the person might have done
something involving an object, allowing
you a larger choice of transitive verbs -
he threw it, he picked it up, he broke it,
he tossed it, he brushed it off, he laid
it down. You might want to become more
specific, describing which parts of his
body moved in the action, or even which
direction he moved in, or how the direction of his movement related to various
other people or objects surrounding him.

If you say this much and no more, you will
get something similar to the script of a
play, with perhaps a few stage directions
included. But, when reading a play, you
can never know the varying intonations,
colorations, emphases, hesitations with
which the actor delivered the lines in the
live theater event. In the same way, a
description of movement, no matter how detailed, when limited to the action itself,
yields little information about how the
mover really moved. You know what he did

but you don't know how he did it. Did he
run with a tight, condensed motion or in
long, free strides? Did he turn abruptly
or very slowly? The thing he picked up -
did he brush it off lightly, or slap his
hand over it, and if he laid it down, did
he just drop it down or was he paying
attention to where he was putting it?

There are many verbs in the language which
combine these two ideas - what someone
does and how he does it. For example, to
fling, toss and hurl are all various ways
to throw something, each with a slightly
different quality. To tap, jab and punch
are different ways of quickly exerting
physical pressure on someone. To pull
something, one may jerk it or tug at it.

Adverbs, such as hurriedly, carefully,
calmly, smoothly, and adjectives like gen-
tle, soft, weak, lively, forceful, are
rich resources for conveying the shades of
movement quality. Below are three para-
graphs, all concerned with the same basic
movement action. The first describes only
the action itself, while the second and
third add qualitative description. The
latter two show only two of hundreds of
possible variations in quality within the
same action.

   -He came down the stairs and stopped,
walked to the door, put his hand on
the knob, turned it and opened the
door.

   -He came bounding down the stairs
and stopped abruptly, walked slowly
and hesitantly to the door, put his

hand firmly on the knob, turned it
fiercely and flung open the door.

-He came softly down the stairs and
stopped, suspended, walked firmly to
the door with a swinging forward
stride and dropped his hand on the
knob, turned it with a tightening
grip and, bracing himself, opened
the door.

An adequate everyday vocabulary serves
perfectly well for describing actions,
both quantitatively and qualitatively, as
long as you have no need for detailed, and
especially for systematic, movement description. Once you begin to observe movement in order to compare, for instance,
two individuals, two cultures, or an individual and a certain standard, you begin
to need descriptive terms which are more
systematic; that is, which point to the
same kinds of qualities each time they are
used; terms which do not overlap in describing phenomena, yet are detailed enough
to describe all the various qualitative
changes which appear in movement.

HISTORY OF EFFORT/SHAPE

A method for systematic description of
qualitative change in movement is a major
product of the life·work of Rudolf Laban
and a number of his co-workers. In this
country it is called Effort Shape. Laban
began his investigation of movement in
Central Europe, where he was involved with
traditional movement forms in ballet and
fencing, with modern forms in developing
the early modern dance style of Central
Europe, and with formalized work movement,

as he used the movement patterns of skilled craftsmen to create large pageants and movement choirs celebrating their skills.

Laban's first attempt to develop a universally applicable movement analysis came in the form of a recording system, Labanotation. Originally, this system was conceived as a description of movement which combined its qualitative and quantitative aspects; eventually however, a situation arose in which the qualitative aspects of movement had to be viewed in a framework of their own.

That situation arose when Laban was asked to do efficiency studies for British industry during World War II. Out of this investigation came a book, Effort, in which Laban and a colleague, F.C. Lawrence, discussed the factors involved in changes in movement quality. Effort, the translation from the German Antrieb, was the name Laban gave to changes which the workers made in the quality of their exertion in movement. Later, another Laban co-worker, Warren Lamb, pursuing aptitude assessment in industrial management in England, formulated the concept of Shape as the correlate of Effort. His concept was largely drawn from the affinities of certain effort qualities with specific dimensions of space which were discussed by Laban in his Choreutics, a study of space harmony. Lamb introduced a set of symbols for shape based on these affinities which correlated the effort symbols with the adaptations of the body in space which were significant for his aptitude measurements. Thus,

Effort/Shape became a method of describing changes in movement quality in terms of the kinds of exertions and the kinds of body adaptations in space.

When Irmgard Bartenieff began to teach these concepts in New York City, a number of specialized applications of Laban's ideas had already begun in England. In addition to Warren Lamb's Effort/Shape system for aptitude assessment, Marion North had begun to apply the concepts, not as Effort/Shape but as Effort, with other considerations including Space, Body, Context, to the assessment of personality, especially with children. Lisa Ullmann, Valerie Preston Dunlop, and many others had developed the Laban concepts into what is called Art of Movement, an educational dance approach that has gained widespread use in the primary schools of England.

Those who have been trained by Irmgard Bartenieff in New York have retained Warren Lamb's term, Effort/Shape, although many do not adhere strictly to his organ-ization of the Effort concepts. Other Effort-trained specialists in this country, notably Betty Meredith-Jones, Diane Davis, Valerie Hunt and others, refer to their work in different ways, according to their own applications of the ideas. For the most part, however, regardless of what they are called, applications of Effort theory remain related to one another, drawing from and contributing to a common frame-work of ideas, although the organization and degree of detail may change from field to field.

THE EFFORT/SHAPE METHOD

Now you have a general picture of the way this system of describing movement quality developed, a system which will be called Effort/Shape from now on. You also know that describing movement in terms of its quality is different from describing the action itself, whether the action is described in everyday terms, such as, he raised his arm; or in the more technical terms of Labanotation - his right arm moved in the direction side-high in 2 seconds (or 2 beats).

The next question must be - how can all the richness and variation in quality in the ongoing stream of human movement be described fully·with a limited number of terms? First of all, you will begin to see this ongoing stream as a series of changes in quality. You will look for the moments when the quality of the stream changes. Then you will see that there are a limited number of things that change. You will see changes in the quality of the body weight, in the sense of time the mover uses; you will see the mover's attention concentrate in space and withdraw from space. You will see the tension of the body changing in quality. You will notice that the body sometimes adapts itself clearly to creating forms in space and sometimes is concerned only with enlarging or condensing its own size. You may notice that the movement repeatedly goes in certain directions, or that it favors certain body parts or always seems to begin from the same place.

And you will see all these ingredients constantly combining with one another, preceding and following one another, reappearing and disappearing. You will learn to recognize these changes in terms of irreducible elements or qualities, and to see that the same kinds of elements, because of their inclusion or exclusion, their combinations, sequences and frequencies of use produce the infinite variety of human movement.

EFFORT

HOW THE BODY CONCENTRATES ITS EXERTION

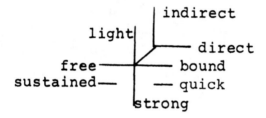

E F F O R T

HOW THE BODY CONCENTRATES ITS EXERTION

When someone moves, you perceive it as
more than a change of place or a change in
the mover's body shape. Movement does not
flow along in a monotone - you see swell-
ings and subsidings, quick flashes, im-
pacts, changes in focus, suspensions,
pressures, flutterings, vigorous swings,
explosions of power, quiet undulations.
All this variety is determined by the way
in which the mover concentrates his exertion or effort. This exertion or effort
may, at any particular moment, be concentrated in the changes in the quality of
the tension, or the flow of movement; it
may be concentrated in changing the quality of the weight, or the quality of time
in the movement; or it may be concentrated
in the mover's focus in space. Flow,
weight, time and space are called Effort
factors. Qualitative change concentrated
in each factor occurs in a range between
two opposite extremes. Each of the extremes is called an element or quality.

The Effort factors are always present in
movement as quantities. Any movement always involves a certain amount of tension
and a quantity of weight; it takes time
and travels in or occupies a certain
amount of space. But when the mover concentrates on changing the quality of any
of these factors, you observe it as an
appearance of one of the eight effort
qualities. Thus the changes in the flow
of tension can be either free or bound;
the quality of the weight can become
either light or strong: the quality of
time can become either sustained or quick
and the quality of the spatial focus or
attention, either indirect or direct.

A useful way of describing these elements
or qualities is to speak of the mover's
attitude toward the Effort factors; e.g.,
someone might have a light attitude toward
weight or an indirect attitude toward
space. These qualities may also be thought
of as ways of coping with or dealing with
or controlling the Effort factors. Here,
"attitude toward" or "control over" or
"coping with" are not meant as something
necessarily conscious that the mover de-
cides to do and does. Movement quality is
an aspect of behavior and can be considered
a product of learning, metabolism, perception of the environment, whatever your
particular bias is about what produces
differences in behavior.

THE FLOW FACTOR*

CHANGES IN THE QUALITY OF THE FLOW OF

TENSION BECOMING EITHER FREE OR BOUND

The alive human body is always in a more
or less "energized" state. Therefore, it
is not really accurate to think of the
polarities of motion as extreme "tension"
and "relaxation" as in a dead flop. The
rhythmic changes in breathing, the constant
responding of the body to both inner and
outer stimuli, provide a constant stream
of urges to move. Thus, when we describe
movement, we must look at it from the beginning as the natural state of the alive
human body. This is particularly important in understanding the "opposite" or
extremes in quality in the flow factor.

---

*The flow factor is usually called "effort
flow," to distinguish it from shape flow,

As you watch a person moving, you may notice that he either holds back, restricts,
binds the flow of his movement, or that he
goes with the flow, his body moving freely
and easily with the motion. The "going
with" the flow of movement we call free;
the restriction of the flow we call bound.
Free and bound are the elements or qualities of the flow factor.

Bound flow is similar to what we very
often call "tense;" free flow to "relaxed."
However, both free and bound flow require
muscular tension; all movement requires
tensing of muscles, and it is the relationship among the muscles tensed, rather
than the presence of tension in the body,
which determines the quality of the flow.

It is a mistake to think that free flow
is "better" than bound flow, even though

---

i.e., the flow of changes in the body
shape (see part II). "Tension flow" is a
term coined by Dr. Judith Kestenberg. It
is used here because it seems to describe
more specifically what it is that is flow-
ing, i.e., the changes in tension in the
body, than does the term effort flow. Dr.
Kestenberg defines tension flow as comple-
mentary (free flow) or opposing (bound
flow) relationships between agonist and
antagonist muscles groups, which is a technical way of saying that it is not the
presence of tension but the quality of the
tension which makes movement flow freely
or with boundness.

the connotations of these terms may suggest
such a value judgment. There are no good
or bad movement qualities as such; there
are appropriate and inappropriate uses of
qualities. The proverbial "bull in the
china shop" is an example, at least in
part, of an inappropriate use of free flow.
Most people find that they must restrict
the flow of their movement in such tasks
as threading a needle or carrying a pot of
hot coffee.

Examples of changing between free and bound
flow might be found in: 1) a free sweep
of your arm during a conversation, in which
you knock something over, and then freeze;
2) carrying a full pan of water over a distance, setting it down and then shaking
yourself for relief.

Although the flow factor is sometimes
viewed as the same "kind" of event on the
same level with the factors of weight,
space and time, it is more often seen in
a slightly different light from the other
Effort factors. Changes in the quality of
flow seem to be the most frequent kind of
changes in movement of all the Effort elements. They seem, in fact, to provide a
kind of substrate in movement, out of
which changes in the qualities of weight,
time and space can "crystallize," as high-
lights among the continuing flow changes.
For example, a boxer in the ring, in between punches, constantly moves his arms,
legs and trunk to keep the flow "alive" or
changing, and out of this he crystallizes
a strong-direct-quick punch. Many conver-
sational gestures are prepared and concluded with flow changes, while elements
of the weight, space and time factors may

emphasize the main statement. From this point of view, flow "feeds" the other factors in a sense, and can be subsumed by the other factors when other qualities crystallize.

ATTRIBUTES OF FLOW

If we look at flow as continuous changes within a range from free to bound, we find that it is useful to distinguish some aspects of the way in which these changes occur.

Dr. Judith Kestenberg, who has developed a method of writing these continuous changes on a curve, as shown below, has developed three sets of characteristics of the way in which the flow changes. She calls them attributes of flow. The first attribute is intensity. Intensity is a term used in relation to all the effort elements. Its approximate meaning is the relative degree of concentration in the production of a quality.* For any effort quality we distinguish three degrees of intensity: extreme or high, middle, and neutral. For tension flow, Dr. Kestenberg speaks of the degrees of intensity of flow, whether free or bound, as high, low and neutral. An example of a change from high

---

*The definition of "intensity" is not to be understood here as quantifiable amount, but as observable change in the degree of a quality, which can be agreed upon by observers.

intensity bound flow to high intensity free flow might be seen in a person holding back mounting emotion and suddenly "flying off the handle," flinging himself around. A change from low intensity bound flow to low intensity free flow might appear in a person carefully removing a drop of ketchup from his clothing and dropping it casually into a container. Neutral flow, either free or bound, might appear in a person's small disheartened shrug.

The next attribute concerns the amount of change that appears in the continuity of flow. If there are many changes in the flow quality, it is characterized as fluctuating.* If the quality of the flow remains very much the same over a period of time, the flow is characterized as even. You might see an example of very fluctuating flow in any discotheque, while even flow is often produced when people attempt to move in "slow motion," or to keep something from spilling.

Finally, Dr. Kestenberg characterizes the duration of change of the flow quality as abrupt or gradual. An abrupt change from free to bound flow might appear in someone reaching for something rather easily and abruptly hesitating as he sees a cockroach on the object he is reaching for. An example of a gradual change from high

---

*Dr. Kestenberg speaks more specifically of these fluctuations in flow as a series of "flow adjustments."

intensity bound flow to low intensity
bound flow might occur in a person very
upset but holding it back, being calmed
by someone. Such a person might breathe
out very gradually, with a long sigh,
losing a certain amount, but not all, of
his "tension."

NOTATION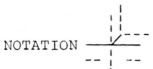

The symbols for free and bound flow are:
⟋ free ∠ bound. The changes between free and bound flow may be written
in symbols distinguishing six degrees on
a range between free and bound:

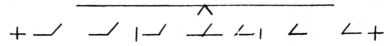

$+$ ⟋ ⟋ |⟋ ∠ ∠| ∠ ∠$+$

"Extreme" and "neutral" correspond to the
attribute of intensity above.

A more detailed way of writing continuous
changes in flow is Dr. Kestenberg's flow
curve. The horizontal axis is measurable
time, the vertical axis intensity.

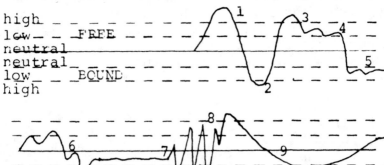

The flow curve above is "hypothetical,"
that is, not based on a real movement pattern but designed to illustrate the six
flow attributes. Numbers 1, 2 and 3 above
show changes from high intensity free to
high intensity bound to high intensity
free; 4 shows low intensity free, 5 low
intensity bound; 6 shows much fluctuation;
7 shows even flow; 8 illustrates abrupt
changes in flow; 9 is a graded change from
low intensity free to low intensity bound
flow.

THE WEIGHT FACTOR

CHANGES IN THE QUALITY OF THE BODY WEIGHT,

BECOMING EITHER LIGHT OR FORCEFUL

Suppose you begin to swing your arm. As
you swing it, you feel not only the flow
of the swing, but the weight of the arm,
its relationship to the pull of gravity.
You might want to change the quality of
the weight, and to do so in such a way as
not to give in to the weight, but to produce an active change in the weight quality. You can change in one of two ways.
Either you can increase the pressure of
that weight, get behind it and push it,
producing a forceful or strong quality of
the weight, or you can withhold, withdraw,
rarify the feeling of the weight, producing a quality of lightness. You might feel,
in this particular action, a swing, that
it is easiest to use force in the middle
of the swing, as the arm moves downward,
and that the feeling of lightness comes
easiest at the ends of the swing with the
upward motion. <u>Light</u> and <u>strong</u> are the

elements or qualities of the weight factor.

If you have a heavy object to move, a heavy carton or a piece of furniture, you may have to engage your weight using a forceful quality. If you lean against the object, giving in to your body weight, the object may not budge. Probably you will have to get behind your weight and really push. On the other hand, if the object you must move is a delicate and breakable one, such as a paper flower, or a thin wire sculpture, you will have to withhold the full weight of your body parts from crushing the object as you move it - your attitude toward your weight will necessarily be one of lightness.

As you observe changes in the quality of weight in people around you, you may find that people sometimes deal with themselves, with one another or with many objects as if they were either large pieces of furniture or delicate paper flowers. You might see examples of strength in a conversation where someone makes his point by supporting his statements with the impact of his body weight in gesturing. Someone who "feels strongly" or takes a "firm stand" probably does so by many repeated instances of the quality of strength in his accompanying movement. Lightness might appear in someone who gently and carefully helps an old lady across the street. Examples of strength in the beginning, middle and end of a movement phrase might appear respectively in a yank on a rope, a tennis serve, chopping a piece of wood. Tasks you might do with lightness include collating papers, where each sheet must be

skimmed off the top of a pile; picking up
splinters of broken glass, fluffing out the
gauzy layers of a tutu.

CONCEPTS RELATED TO THE WEIGHT FACTOR

Sensation of weight - Effort-Shape does not
describe perceptions or sensations, but
only movement patterns which may result
from these. Although sensation of weight
is not part of Effort description per se,
it is a condition without which the qualities of lightness and strength cannot
occur. A mover must be able clearly to
sense his own body weight before he can
actively change its quality.

Center of weight or center of gravity -
The center of weight refers to the part of
the body most involved in initiating shifts
of weight and generally activating and supporting the body weight, i.e., the pelvis.
Activation of the center of weight is necessary for producing changes in the quality
of the weight, either light or strong.
Center of levity is a term sometimes used
to refer to the upper trunk and more specifically to the sternum. Activation in
the chest, sternum, ribs and upper back,
with support from the lower trunk, provide
optimum conditions for producing lightness.

Shift of weight - Shifting the weight is
a phrase used to describe the body weight
when it changes place or support, no matter
how slightly. Although a shift of weight
is a change in weight distribution, it is
not necessarily change in the quality of
the weight, so that one may speak of a
weight shift without necessarily bringing
in strength and lightness.

Heaviness - Heaviness is often confused
with strength, and heavy is thought of as
the opposite of light. "Heavy" and "light"
as opposites, however, describe the condition of objects or people who are acted
upon - lifted, carried, etc. - while a person who actively changes his weight quality in movement can best be described in
terms of strong and light. Heaviness appears in movement as giving in to gravity,
in tired, floppy movement, or sometimes in
momentum swings when the weight is sensed
but not yet actively strong. It is a useful descriptive term, but in Effort-Shape
it is not the opposite of light, nor the
same as strong.

NOTATION

The symbols for lightness and strength are:
light   strong. . As in the notation
of flow, degrees of intensity may be noted
by adding " - " for slight or neutral, or
a " + " for exaggerated, at the outside of
each symbol.

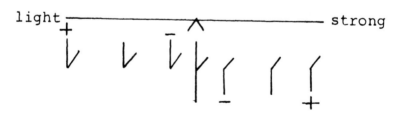

THE TIME FACTOR

CHANGES IN THE QUALITY OF TIME IN

MOVEMENT, BECOMING EITHER SUSTAINED

OR QUICK

Scene: gangster movie. Rich industrialist whose daughter has been kidnapped con-
fronting mobster he knows is responsible.
Where is his daughter - he wants to know
now. Well . . . mobster isn't quite sure,
is stalling for time to make sure his plans
have been carried out. Industrialist's
movements are punctuated with quick, ner-
vous jerks and starts. Mobster smokes his
cigar with long sustained gestures, stretching out every second as much as he can.

The dynamic in this scene consists in opposing attitudes toward time. The two men
share the same duration in their exchange;
they exist and interact in the same amount
of time. But the one acts from a sense of
urgency, of wanting to hurry time, while
the other indulges in time, as if prolonging its passage. The quality of prolonging

or stretching time out, we call sustainment the quality of urgency or quick-
ening in time we call quick
Sustained and quick are the elements or
qualities of the time factor.*

The qualities of sustainment and quickness
differ from quantitative speed as measured
by a clock, or pace or tempo as marked by
a metronome. In ballet, or more extremely
in Spanish dance, the legs and feet may be
moving in response to very fast-paced music,
while in the arms and upper body, the quality of sustainment in time may appear. An
instance of the quality of quickness in
contrast to clocked speed might appear in a
runner at the starting line of a dash. The
runner anticipates the signal to start, has
a growing attitude of urgency in time, then
at the signal, he makes a quick start,
after which he may maintain a fast pace by
means of other elements, such as flow,
strength, directness.

Sustainment - - -   is also different
from slow motion in most cases. If a dancer or actor has to remain in slow motion
for a period of time, he soon forgets
about changes in the quality of time alto-

---

*Some observers, notably Dr. Kestenberg,
and Warren Lamb, use the terms "accelera-
tion and deceleration" rather than quick
and sustained. They are still not refer-
ring to measurable changes in rate of
speed, but to qualitative changes toward
sustainment in movement.

gether. He has all he can do to hold back
the natural tendencies of the movement to
flow rhythmically rather than evenly.
Thus, most slow-motion becomes an exercise
in maintaining even, bound flow, and has
little to do with the mover's sense of
time. You would be more likely to see the
quality of sustainment in dance at the
height of a lift in ballet or in an off
balance suspension, where the dancer keeps
the motion going by drawing out, sustaining
the time before the pull of gravity has its
way.

The relationship between the movement
qualities of quickness and sustainment,
and the quantitative measurement of fast
and slow, is, essentially, that quickness
will probably be used to heighten patterns
that are fast-paced and sustainment will
likely be used to accompany slow-paced
patterns. But quickness   and
sustainment are qualities which can occur
and be observed when "speed" is irrelevant
and/or impossible to measure. For example,
a person may be very slow-paced about inch-
ing his way along a narrow path on a high
cliff, but if he begins to lose his balance,
he will assuredly punctuate this slow-
paced movement with sudden jerks to regain
his balance. On the other hand, a quick-
paced, animated conversation may include
moments of hesitation, of slow, gradual,
drawn-out changes within a fast-paced
rhythm.

NOTATION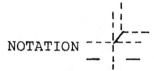

The symbols for sustainment and quickness
are: /   sustained /   quick   As
in the other factors, intensity can be
noted by adding "—" for slight or neutral
and a "+" for exaggerated at the ends of
the symbols.

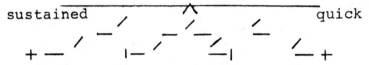

sustained   quick

THE SPACE FACTOR

CHANGES IN THE QUALITY OF SPATIAL FOCUS

OR ATTENTION, BECOMING EITHER INDIRECT

OR DIRECT

You may have noticed at various times that
when people interact with you they can focus attention on you in more than one way.
In a discussion, say, when it is necessary
for a person really to "take you in," to
pay attention to you as you stand or sit
before him, in order to communicate something to you, he might pinpoint or channel
his attention on you directly, "zeroing in"
on you with a single focus. Or he might
take you in from various angles, keeping
his attention scanning around you, allowing
his body to move among a number of spatial
approaches to you, or foci that continuously overlap. Here, his spatial focus appears constantly flexible, sometimes
"roundabout" - we call it indirect.

Or, at some time you may have had occasion
to be in a dark room and be startled by a
noise in the room. How did you begin to
pay attention to where the noise came
from? If you knew exactly where it was,
you might have suddenly directed your
whole body into a single focus on that
spot. If you weren't sure where it came
from, you might have found, in observing
yourself, that various parts of your body
were each focusing within, or taking in
a different area of the room.

Movement in which spatial attention consists of overlapping shifts in the body
among a number of foci, we call indirect.
Movement in which spatial attention in
the body is pinpointed, channelled,
single focused, we call direct. Indirect
and direct are the elements or qualities
of the space factor.

Visual contact with an object is not always an indication of indirectness and
directness. You may occasionally see
these qualities appear in a person when
he is not attentive to the space around
him, but is imagining, or remembering, or
seeing something in his mind. For example,
in Western movies, the cowboy often finds
himself with his hands tied behind him.
In order to free himself, he pictures in
his mind the way the rope is tied, or
where a sharp object lies on a table behind him. He cannot "see" the space he is
dealing with, but he may focus his attention on the way he pictures it, and, as a
result, may approach the space directly

or indirectly. Or in another case, a person may be concentrating on remembering
how a particular tune goes. In his accompanying gestures, he may search in his
mind, following the tune along with indirectness, then zero in on the missing note
with directness.

To get through a crowd of people, you
might have to ease your way through by
distributing yourself into may small available openings at once, using indirectness,
or you may see a narrow lane where you can
dash through quickly if you channel yourself with directness.

The elements of indirectness and directness
are often confused with certain aspects of
movement shape, namely directional and
shaping movement. While the effort qualities are concerned with the kind of concentration or focus in space, the shape
aspects of movement are more related to
pathways and forms the body parts create
in space. We will save this problem for
Part II.

NOTATION

The symbols for indirect and direct are:

indirect /⎯ direct. Like the
other effort symbols, these can denote
varying degrees of intensity by the addition of the "-" or " +".

indirect ⎯⎯⎯⎯⎯⎯⎯⎯⎯⎯⎯⎯⎯ direct

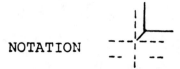

EFFORT - SOME THEORETICAL CONSIDERATIONS

We have examined four Effort factors and,
for each factor, two elements which can be
regarded as polarities in a range within
which the quality of each factor may be
changed. Thus, the factor of weight may
change in quality toward lightness or
strength, the factor of flow toward boundness or freeness, and so on.

You can think of the four factors of flow,
weight, time and space as the four ingredients of movement upon which it is possible to concentrate your exertion or effort.
Laban sometimes referred to these factors
as the how, what, when and where of movement; his "how" refers to the way the
movement flows, "what" to the weight factor, "when" to time, and "where" to space.
From this perspective, a person moving
without particular awareness of "what"
was moving would be unlikely to produce
lightness or strength; a person paying
little attention to "when" would probably
lack sustainment or quickness in his movement.

Dr. Judith Kestenberg, whose point of view
regarding Effort is influenced by her research in child development, adds a different interpretive emphasis. She sees
changes in the flow factor as affording
control over oneself, or over the changes
in tension in one's own body, while changes
concentrated on weight, space and time
afford control within the environment.
Thus a person, at least in the beginning
of his life, attends to changes in flow to
facilitate bodily functions such as inges-
tion, elimination, etc., while to push
something away, he must do something to
his weight, or to get around something, he
must attend to his approach to space. Between coping with oneself and coping with
the environment, Dr. Kestenberg finds that
there are various times when a certain way
of coping with oneself is related to a way
of dealing with the environment. In other
words, certain characteristics of flow,
namely the attributes, are related to certain effort qualities. These relationships
are as follows: high intensity free or
bound flow is related to strength, low intensity free or bound flow is related to
lightness; a gradual change in the quality
(or intensity) of flow is related to sustainment, an abrupt change to quickness
a lot of fluctuation in the flow is related to indirectness; no fluctuation in
flow, or evenness, to directness.

Just as Dr. Kestenberg has gone into great
detail in observing flow, other practitioners use varying degrees of detail in looking at other Effort factors. Earlier, you
read that, for example, changing the

quality of the weight could be thought of
as occurring within a range from extremely
light to extremely strong. For most observation, you will note only what is extremely strong, or strong, and not pay
much attention to what is a little strong
or almost strong. But sometimes an element
remains present, as when someone remains
in a certain state, and you may want to
observe all its changes from "maybe" and
"sort of" to "extremely" and "very." For
example, the figure of Death in Kurt Jooss'
The Green Table exudes the quality of
strength from his first appearance on the
stage, and never loses it during the dance.
He stomps violently or presses slowly forward or carries someone firmly or fights
forcefully. In short, he uses many shades
of strength and combines strength with
other qualities but he never loses it al-
together.

Now if your concern in observing movement
is with how many elements are used and how
many changes are made from one element to
another, you will note one appearance of
strength when Death makes his first movement and you will never note it again
because he never loses his strength and
has to recreate it. But if you are inter-
ested in watching the flow of strength,
much as Dr. Kestenberg observes the flow
of tension, then you will note the varying
degrees of strength, what other elements
it combines with, i.e., the flow of changes
within the element itself.

In other words, some observers look more
at changes among Effort elements, for how
many times they are recreated in movement,

while others look for changes within elements, how they diminish and intensify and
combine with other elements. Clearly then,
once you become familiar with these factors
and the elements which are their changes in
quality, there is more than one way to look
at their appearance in the stream of movement.

Another kind of perspective from which to
regard the Effort factors is illustrated
by examining the grid which Laban used to
represent the Effort concept.

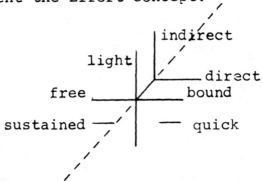

If the diagonal line which relates the
symbols is extended, a kind of division
is produced. The elements to the left of
the diagonal - indirectness, lightness,
freeness, sustainment - share a characteristic property of rarifying or spreading out, going along with, indulging.
Thus one could think of indirectness as
spreading out in or going along with indulging in space, or lightness as rarifying or spreading out the weight, of freeness as going along with or indulging in
the flow of movement; of sustainment as
spreading out of or indulging in time.

The elements to the right of the diagonal
share a kind of condensing or fighting
character. Directness can be seen as condensing in or fighting space, in the sense
of channeling it; boundness as fighting
the flow of movement; quickness as fighting
or condensing time, compressing it;
strength as condensing the weight into
force.

These, then, are some of the perspectives
from which you can view the Effort factors
as a group. They are included here not as
researched statements of fact nor as pure
speculation, but to suggest possible implications and applications of Effort concepts.

EFFORT ELEMENTS IN COMBINATION

When Laban began to formalize his concept
of Effort, he was involved in observing
patterns of workers in the British war industry. Work which physically involves
the worker, be he farmer, bricklayer,
welder, longshoreman, or high-powered ex-
ecutive, demands from him a great deal in
terms of his organization of his effort or exertion. Very often, the problems he en-
counters are more than only weight-lifting
or only spatial exactness; in fact, the
worker is often required to attend to
weight, space and time simultaneously.
Laban found moments in movement when attention to the demands of weight, space and
time take over or subsume ongoing changes
in flow. Simultaneous concentration on
the three factors of weight, space and
time, Laban called "Basic Effort Actions";
they are also sometimes referred to as
"full efforts."

There are eight possible combinations of
one element each from weight, space and

time, to each of which Laban gave a name,
an everyday action term. The eight are:

FLOAT	WRING	PRESS	GLIDE
indirect	indirect	direct	direct
light	strong	strong	light
sustained	sustained	sustained	sustained

DAB	FLICK	SLASH	PUNCH
direct	indirect	indirect	direct
light	light	strong	strong
quick	quick	quick	quick

In many minds, the eight basic effort
actions have become synonymous with Effort
as a system, but in fact, these basic
actions constitute the most highly crystallized exertions described in the system
rather than its basic 'ingredients. If you
attempt to produce the eight full efforts,
not simply by doing what the everyday terms
suggest in each case, but by actively
changing the quality of your weight, your
spatial attention and your attitude toward
time - all at once - you will experience
how much concentration and active partici-

pation they require of you. This kind of
concentration is different from that of
deep meditation or strong feeling of yourself. It is seen as arousing you to
action, as in working, fighting, involving
yourself in intense interaction with people and objects.

Laban called the basic effort actions as a
group the "action drive," where each action
combined elements from the weight, space
and time factors. When two of these three
factors appeared combined with flow, he
referred to these combinations also as
various kinds of "drives." The combination
of flow, space and time, where concentration on weight is absent, Laban called the
"vision drive." This drive he refers to
as "weightless" and "reduced in bodily im-
port." The combination of flow, space,
and weight, where change in the quality of
time is absent, he called the "spell drive,"
where, he says, the "movements radiate a
quality of fascination." Flow, combined
with weight and time, where there is no
attitude toward space, Laban called the
"passion drive," where "bodily actions are
particularly expressive of emotion and
feeling."*

Aside from those in the action drive, Laban
never named specifically each of the combinations of three qualities. In part,
this may be because language can be more
exacting about action than it can be in
supplying terms for subtle shades of less

*All descriptions in quotation marks taken
from Laban's Mastery of Movement, p. 85.

externalized experiences. A detailed out-
line of the possible combinations of elements in each of these four drives is included in the appendix. Further verbal
discussion and speculation about these
combinations is unproductive without ex-
periencing in movement the differences
among the combinations.

Combinations of elements from two factors
attended to simultaneously are as elusive
to language as those combining three factors at once. Laban referred to combinations from two factors as "incomplete
effort," a term which compares them by
the number of factors combined, with the
four drives. An alternative way of describing combinations of two elements is
"inner attitudes," which suggests that the
movement statement is not yet externalized,
but expresses various moods and states of
feeling. Of these "incomplete efforts,"
Laban said, "It is difficult to attach
names to these variations of incomplete
effort as they are concerned with pure
movement experience and expression."*

There are six ways in which the effort
factors can be combined in groups of two.
Thus, movement involving these "inner
attitudes" may be concentrated in space
and time or weight and flow, in space and
flow or weight and time, in space and
weight or time and flow. Laban originally
characterized these combinations respectively as awake, dreamlike, remote, near,
stable, mobile. But again, understanding

*Ibid, p. 86.

of these combinations will arise from movement experience alone. The verbal description is perhaps less than precise and sub-
ject to variation according to context.
Within each combination of two factors, you
can combine the elements in four different
ways; for example, movement concentrated in
space and time might appear as indirect-
sustained, indirect-sudden, direct-sustained,
or direct-sudden. All possible combinations
within the six groupings are outlined in
the appendix.*

The importance of the combinations of effort
elements for movement observation in general is in seeing what elements people combine
in movement. A clown, for instance, pre-
tending to fight, might punch, missing his
target and being knocked off his feet by
his own momentum. The clown, creating his
humor by inappropriate movement, combines
flow with weight and time in his punch, instead of space, which is what his audience
expects. That is, his audience expects
him to direct his strength suddenly toward
his target, rather than to do as he does -
let it flow out suddenly without channeling
it. A clown, as part of his skill, may
choose such a combination to serve an

*Marion North, in England, has done the
most extensive work with the "inner attitudes" and with the drives, which she calls
"externalized drives." You are referred
to her Personality Assessment Through
Movement (MacDonald & Evans) London,
available June 1970. Because so little investigation has been done in this area in
the U.S., I can do little more than quote
existing sources concerning these combinations.

expressive function in his performance. However, people in general select certain combinations of elements as part of their individual differences in behavior. Selection of different combinations figures largely in what you recognize as one dance style or another. A person may actively change the quality of his weight only if he has at the same time a clear attention to space. Or a person may more readily change the quality of time if he restricts the flow of his movement. In short, it is not merely the presence or absence of the factors of weight, time, space and flow, but the many ways in which their elements combine that provides the endless variety of dynamics with which people move.

S H A P E

HOW THE BODY FORMS ITSELF IN SPACE

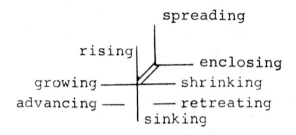

spreading

rising

enclosing

growing —— shrinking

advancing — —— retreating

sinking

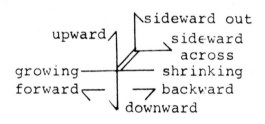

sideward out

upward

sideward across

growing —— shrinking

forward backward

downward

S H A P E

HOW THE BODY FORMS ITSELF IN SPACE

In the first part of this text we have
viewed the movement process in terms of
how the mover concentrates his exertion or
effort. Yet, from the beginning, in order
to look in detail at changes in exertion,
we have already been seeing the movement
process from a certain level of abstraction.
That is, by speaking only of changes in
exertion, we have abstracted this concept
from other aspects which figure as part of
the ongoing process of movement.

This will become clear to you if you
attempt just to charge your body with an
effort or exertion, whatever its quality.

Immediately something else happens. Your
body makes a change, no matter how slight,
in its relationship among its parts and to
the surrounding space. The effort, from
the beginning, has a form, takes a shape.
Just as you have begun to discern different

ways of concentrating the movement exertion, you will now begin to see that
changes in form in movement may be simi-
larly differentiated.

We will distinguish three kinds of change
in the form of movement: 1) shape flow -
where the form results only from changes
within the body parts; 2) directional movement - where the form results from a clear
path going in a direction in space;
3) shaping movement - where the form results from the body clearly molding itself
in relation to the shape of space, whether
it creates the shape of the space, as in
dance, or adapts to it, as in many work
movements.

S H A P E   F L O W

CHANGES IN THE BODY PARTS TOWARD OR AWAY

FROM THE BODY CENTER

When movement involves a change of relationship of one, several or all of the
parts of the body, it can be seen from
either of two perspectives, both of which
can be called shape flow. The first of
these emphasizes either total body or torso where the body can be said to grow or
shrink.

An example of growing in the body might
appear in someone taking a deep breath
and stretching to fill his lungs. Shrinking might occur in someone who contracts
his body as he shouts, or in someone sigh-
ing with relief as he slumps in a chair.
The most basic model for shape flow, when
it is seen as growing and shrinking, is
the inflation and deflation of the trunk
in breathing. A breathing pattern which
is full and continuous, without holding,
promotes the flow of shape changes in the
body.

The other perspective from which one can
describe shape flow emphasizes the limbs.
In this case, a change in the flow of shape
can be described as folding or closing toward the center, or unfolding, opening out
from the center. The terms in and out or
toward and away may be substituted when
they are more appropriate.

Shape flow described as opening and closing is a useful concept for basic, total
body movements, especially in lying or
sitting. Someone who sits up from lying,
hugging his knees to his chest, may be described as folding, or closing up, while
someone who spreads himself on the floor
from sitting may be said to open or unfold.
If you watch everyday conversations you
may see people alternating among patterns
of opening and closing, appearing to close
themselves away from the conversation, or
open themselves up to it. Very often, one
part of the body may close while another
opens, as when someone folds his arms and
at the same time assumes a wide stance.

Whether you use the concept of shape flow
as growing and shrinking or as opening and
closing, it applies to movement in which
the form is dictated by a concern with the
relationship within the parts of the body,
i.e., it is body-oriented, and is not concerned primarily with the space around the
body. This will become clearer when you
compare shape flow with the concepts of
directional movement and shaping.

When you look at movement to observe the
flow of shape, you may want to be more

specific about the <u>reach space</u> within which
the movement occurs. The concept of reach
space distinguishes how close to or far
away from the body movement takes place.
Three obvious areas of reach are discrimin-
ated: near reach, intermediate reach and
far reach. Near reach, in the arms, for
example, is the area very close to the
body, where sewing or knitting is often
done. Intermediate reach is approximately
the distance from elbow (close to the body)
to the fingertips extended away from the
body, the area in which much gesturing is
done. Far reach is the full extent of the
whole arm out from the body, without locomotion. The limits of far reach are the
limits of what Laban called the personal
kinesphere, i.e., the space around the
body which can be reached without taking
a step. Reach space as a concept is useful for describing various dance styles,
work movement, interaction in theater or
everyday movement.

NOTATION:

The symbols denoting shape flow, whichever
of the above terms one uses, are:

growing, unfolding,   shrinking, folding,
opening, out, away   closing, in, toward

Dr. Judith Kestenberg combines the concepts
of shape flow and reach space in writing
shape flow curves, which are similar to her
effort, or tension flow curves. She writes

the shape flow curve along three parallel
lines which divide space into near, intermediate and far reach. She can then record
growing and shrinking continuously whether
it occurs in near, intermediate or far
reach space. The upward slope of the curve
represents growing, the downward slope
shrinking.

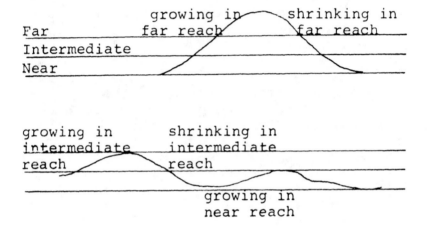

DIRECTIONAL MOVEMENT

SPOKE-LIKE OR ARC-LIKE MOVEMENT "LINKING"
THE BODY WITH A PLACE IN SPACE

Our ideas about the space in which we exist
do not come to us by contemplation of an
empty expanse that recedes from us in all
directions. In fact, if we existed in a
void, the idea of space receding from us
would probably never occur to us. We
learn about space by encountering the objects which define it. Things appear at
various distances from us; they occupy the
space in different directions from the
fronts of our bodies; they occupy more or
less space than our bodies do.

Thus, as you begin to attend to the space
around you, the form of your movement
begins to be determined by more than the
relationship among your body parts. Directional movement appears as the most basic
form in which movement establishes a relationship to the surrounding space. Dr.

Kestenberg refers to directional movement as "establishing a bridge from the mover to an object." What is the form of such a movement-bridge, either to an object or to a point in space or into a general area of space?

If you reach out from yourself toward something around you, or if you reach from one point to another, and you observe the path your body makes in moving, you will find that the path has one of two possible forms. First, the path may have the form of a straight line. Your reaching part may travel along a linear path to get to the point, the part itself moving in a spoke-like manner out from your body. Examples of this directional 'spoke-like movement might appear in someone pushing something forward away from his chest, or in a traffic cop who thrusts his arm out to stop a stream of traffic, or in a catcher who reaches up overhead to catch a ball.

The second possible form the path may take is that of a flat arc through space. That is, if you want to reach something to the side of you, and instead of thrusting your arm out in a spoke-like way, you swing it out from its hanging position, you have described a flat arc in space, called directional arc-like movement. Examples of directional arc-like movement could be seen in the jumping jack exercise in calesthenics, or the arm movement of the boxing referee counting for a knockout. Where spoke-like movment often involves the unfolding of many body parts into a direction, arc-like movement is more likely to be active in only one joint, as for

instance the whole arm moving as a unit
from the shoulder joint.

As you can see from many of the examples,
the motive of reaching for an object,
through which people may learn originally
to form their movement into spoke-like and
arc-like paths, soon becomes abstracted,
so that an object is unnecessary. Only a
clear idea of direction is required to produce these forms in movement. In dance,
where the motivation for movement becomes
even more abstract, directional movement
may be seen in which not only is the object invisible, but the direction or goal
in space is not so important as the form
of the path itself, or the process of
moving through a form. What this means
for observers in the field of dance is
that directional movement in dance often
must be thought of much more in terms of
a spoke-like, linear path, or an arc-like,
flat form, rather than as going toward a
place or thing or point in space. The
latter is much closer to the everyday,
functional appearances of directional
movement.

NOTATION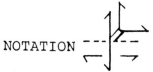

The symbols for directional movement are
given in terms of the cross of axes by
which three dimensional space can be described, where the vertical axis of space
coincides with the body midline.

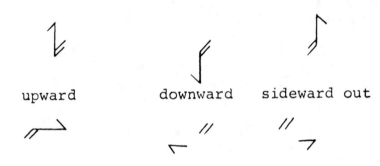

upward   downward   sideward out

sideward across   forward   backward

The symbols are used for all directional
movement, whether spoke-like or arc-like,
although upon occasion you may want to
distinguish these two types of directional
movement, in which case you can improvise
changes with the flags on the symbols.

When a directional movement occurs in a
direction other than one of the six directions which have their own symbols, for
example, in a spoke-like movement going
sideward, forward and upward in the direction forward-side-high, the directional
symbols are combined to denote the move-

ment, i.e.,   which means that the

movement is linear or spoke-like and going
toward a point in space which is forward,
upward, and to the side in relation to the
front of the body.

If you are "making notes," or using a
coding sheet or various other "listing"
processes in observation, it is sometimes

convenient to use the words directional spoke-like or arc-like with the Labanotation symbols (see next section) for the predominant directions the movement goes in.

SHAPING

THE BODY'S CREATING OF OR ADAPTING TO CONTOUR, TO TWO AND THREE DIMENSIONAL FORMS IN SPACE

Suppose you are sitting on the floor and next to you is a large ball, about two feet in diameter. And suppose you have at your disposal all the movement elements we have discussed so far; all the effort elements plus shape flow, the growing (opening) and shrinking (closing) of your body, and directional movement, spoke-like and arc-like. If you begin to play with the ball, you will find that you can open yourself toward it, or close yourself away, that you can reach toward it, push it from place to place with many different dynamics, perhaps even pull it toward you with a spoke-like directional movement backward. But if you begin to allow your hand to spread itself over part of the ball's volume, and especially if you mold your arm around it and allow your trunk to

accomodate to its shape, you are beginning to introduce the quality of shaping
into your movement repertoire.

Shaping is the aspect of movement form
which allows the mover to accommodate to
the plastic character of objects in
space, to their volume, or contour,
their three dimensionality, and conse-
quently to mold space into plastic forms
himself, whether in clay as the sculptor
does, or in thin air, as the dancer,
mime and storyteller do. In shaping,
the active part of the body constantly
adapts to the form of space, whether this
be an already formed object, a person, or
a form being created by the mover. Ana-
tomically speaking, shaping requires the
constant blending of the muscle group
functions in many joints to allow the
body's fullest adaptation.

A person who has piled up sand for building a castle on the beach will begin to
make the form of the pile more specific,
using his hands and arms to round out the
form while the rest of the body adapts to
the needs of the main activity. A person
making his way through a chaotically
cluttered room will mold his body along
in the shape of whatever empty space is
created by the assortment of objects in
the room. A dressmaker draping material
on a mannekin shapes the fabric by ad-
justing her movement to follow the dic-
tates of the material on the mannekin's
form. A cook shapes the wooden spoon
along the inside contour of the bowl. A
parent takes a baby in his arms by molding his own body around the child's shape.

These are all examples containing shaping movement.

CONCEPTS RELATED TO SHAPING:

Gathering and Scattering - When a movement can be said to be shaping, but emphasizes either coming toward the body or going away from the body, rather than any particular directions in space, the terms gathering (shaping towards the body) and scattering (shaping away from the body) may be used to describe the movement. Gathering and scattering are terms as traditionally associated with Laban theory as are basic effort actions such as "punch" and "float." They can be very helpful, evocative terms for directors and movement teachers, who may be looking for general terms for orienting actors and dancers. They are perhaps less useful in detailed notation and research, since gathering and scattering can be broken down into more basic concepts. Sometimes the symbols for shape flow: ___// scattering and //__ gathering, are used to notate this phenomenon, but this depends on the context.

NOTATION

The symbols for shaping, like those for directional movement, are based on the three-dimensional cross of axes; they are the same as the directional symbols but for shaping the flags are omitted. Also note the difference in the terms for shaping and those for directional. The former suggest the emphasis on the body's involvement in forming or adapting to space, while directional terms stress the concern with going in specific directions.

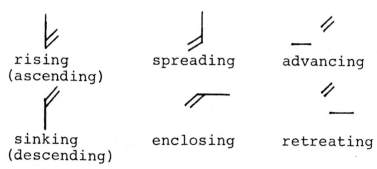

| rising (ascending) | spreading | advancing |
| sinking (descending) | enclosing | retreating |

These symbols were developed by Warren Lamb as a way of describing primarily the concavity or convexity of the torso in terms of the planes or cycles of movement. Thus each symbol represents a predominant cycle rather than a single direction. Rising, spreading and advancing describe convexity of the torso in the vertical, horizontal and sagittal cycles respectively, while sinking, enclosing and retreating describe concavity in these cycles. Rising and sinking occur in the vertical cycles, where shaping that is mainly upward-downward also has a sideward component. Spreading and enclosing occur in the horizontal cycle, where shaping that is mainly sideward across or out away from the body also has a forward-backward component, as in an embrace. Advancing and retreating occur in the sagittal cycle where shaping that is mainly forward and backward also has an upward-downward component.

Although Lamb stresses the use of the torso in shaping, these symbols may also be used to describe limb movement. In a pirouette, for example, where torso movement is minimal, one arm spreads and the other encloses during the turn. Limb and torso movement may or may not involve the same shaping components.

As in directional movement, shaping that involves combinations of rising, spreading etc., may be denoted by combining the symbols. For example, shaping which simultaneously advances, spreads and sinks,

would be symbolized as follows:

Again, if one is merely making notes, or using a coding sheet or other listing device, it is sometimes useful to use the word shaping and indicate by Labanotation symbols or other methods the predominant cycles or areas in which the movement occurs.

SHAPE - SOME THEORETICAL CONSIDERATIONS

All the terms that lie within the category
of shape, whether included in shape flow,
directional or shaping, are concerned with
the form of movement. In some contexts,
the form is defined more in motivational
terms, e.g., establishing a bridge to an
object or adapting to objects in space.
For others, the form is defined more as
design or spatial access, e.g., linear,
planal, plastic, or one-, two- and three-
dimensional. Or a context may stress both
aspects.

Effort, or the concentration of exertion,
and shape, may be said to relate to each
other as "opposite sides of a coin." You
can describe the stream of movement as
continuous changes in effort and continuous
changes in shape. In Effort/Shape notation,
the effort changes are written parallel to
and above the shape changes.

As in all opposites, there is an area of
ideas within which the differences between
effort and shape are not so clear, or not

so polar, and are easily confused. In
Effort/Shape, this area includes the space
factor, the elements of indirectness and
directness, from the effort category, and
the concepts of directional movement and
shaping from the shape category. The dis-
tinction may be clarified by observing in examples whether the mover pays attention
to space, i.e., involves the effort factor
of space, or whether he creates a form in
space, i.e., uses directional movement or
shaping, or whether he does both.

If your attention is attracted to a place
in space, and you concentrate your attention, in your whole body, on that place,
you are producing the effort quality directness, but you have not yet created any
clear spatial path or form. Now you reach
out with your head and trunk toward the
place, perhaps to have a closer look. Now
you are adding a directional form to your
direct attention. Or, on the other hand,
suppose you are trying to lift a heavy
object, concentrating your exertion
in the weight factor, and someone comes
along to ask you where the nearest mailbox
is. Without letting up on the object you
point down the road with a gesture of your
arm without letting your attention change
particularly from the lifting to the place
you are indicating. You have gestured
toward the mailbox with a directional movement but you didn't really pay attention
to the space. In short, it is possible to
be direct with or without directional movement and to use directional movement with
or without directness.

The same relationship is true for the effort quality of indirectness and shaping. Suppose you are standing under a tree you want to climb. You allow your attention, in various body parts, to scan about overhead, looking for a spot where you might get a foothold. You are regarding the tree with indirectness, allowing yourself many foci, many possible approaches. Now you see where you can twist and pull yourself up into the tree. You reach around and up and begin to shape yourself into the tree branches, still keeping your attention moving in overlapping changes of focus. Here you began with indirectness and added shaping to it.

An example of shaping without spatial attention, either indirect or direct, would be difficult to think of and in everyday life probably quite rare, provided the shaping were more than an arm gesture. Probably such shaping is more frequent in Western abstract concert dance, where much of the training concerns producing the form without necessarily equal emphasis on the changing attitudes and feelings accompanying the form, as one would find in dance-drama or drama.

It was noted above that the shape concept can either emphasize what motivates the form or the design aspects of the form itself. The former perspective was implicit in the discussion of how you could deal with a large ball placed beside you. By changing the relationship within your body itself, you would emphasize the shape flow aspect of the shape category, the most rudimentary aspect of shape, a kind

of pre-space adaptation of the body. By
reaching out toward the ball, or rolling
it in any direction, you would use directional movement to establish a bridge between yourself and the ball, or between
directions or places in space where the
ball might move. By grasping the ball,
rounding your arms and body around it, you
would mold yourself, or part of yourself
to the form of the ball with shaping movement.

We can look at this same situation from
the perspective of the character of the
form itself. This perspective has become
formalized mainly through the use of a
coding sheet by the Choreometrics project
of Columbia University, in which Irmgard
Bartenieff and Forrestine Paulay collabor-
ate with Alan Lomax in researching dance
and work styles from many cultures.* Here,
the opening-closing changes within your
body itself would be called vague or inde-
finite, having no clear spatial path or
form. As you reached for the ball, or
rolled it from place to place, your path
might be called linear or flat arc, a one-
or two-dimensional form. As you molded
yourself around the ball, your form might
be called three-dimensional, rounded, perhaps looped or spiraled. (Although these
terms are not all strictly quoted from the
Choreometrics coding sheet, they suggest
its point of view.)

*See Lomax, et al, Folk Song Style and
Culture, AAAS, 1968. See also CORD Proceedings, May 1967, pp. 91-104.

Here the form is described in terms of the
kind of access to space which it allows
the mover. For example, if a person used
only spoke-like directional forms in movement his access to space would be different
from a person who also used loops or
spirals (shaping). The difference would
be both functional and expressive.

Using this perspective, Choreometrics has
distinguished various types of spatial
transition, or ways in which people change
direction, a parameter they have found most
important in comparing movement cross-
culturally. Some kinds of spatial transition, which are special refinements of
shape flow-directional-shaping concepts,
are as follows: 1) vague 2) simple reversal
3) cyclic 4) angular 5) looped.

A term which is easily confused with directional movement and shaping is trace form.
Although it is not part of the Effort/
Shape concepts, you may find it valuable
upon occasion for movement description.
If you are looking at the trace form of a
movement, you are observing the spatial
lines and curves created by the end of a
body part, at the "drawing left in air" as
it were, while you are not then concerned
with observing the kind of bodily adaptation that may create the form. The latter
is important in the concepts of direction-
ality and shaping.

Finally, in the same way that effort qualities do not often appear and remain
throughout a whole movement phrase, so
shape flow, directional movement and shaping occur in various proportions and

sequences in movement phrases. Lively
shape flow, like effort flow, can "feed"
the production of the clear spatial forms
(directional and shaping movement). For
example, in ballet movement, very subtle
growing and shrinking changes must occur
in the trunk to support the complex directional movement of the arms and legs -
otherwise the movement looks rigid and
mechanical. On the other hand, in traditional modern dance, where the movement is
often motivated by large changes in the
trunk with the limbs following, the whole
body may become involved in shaping, and
the shape flow becomes subsumed. In the
action of a tennis serve, the mover may
prepare with shape flow toward himself ⟋— ,
shape on the backward swing as he tosses

the ball. ⎵ (retreating, rising, spreading

become directional as the ball is hit ⟋

(forward, downward, across), and return in
the follow-through to shape flow toward
himself ⟋—.

EFFORT SHAPE

DIAGRAM OF NOTATION AND INTERRELATIONSHIPS
AMONG QUALITIES

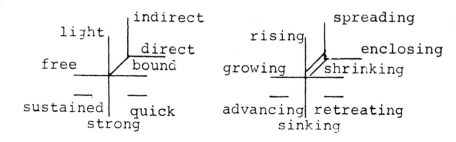

1. This diagram shows all the notation symbols for effort elements and shape flow
   and shaping. The diagonal line which
   is repeated with each symbol indicates
   that a change has occurred in movement.
   The single diagonal line indicates a
   change in effort; the double diagonal
   a change in shape. What kind of change
   in effort or shape is indicated by which
   of the lines extending from the diagon-
   als above is noted. Directional

movement is indicated by adding flags
to the shape symbols.

2. Free and bound effort flow and growing
   and shrinking in shape flow are considered different order terms from the
   effort elements and the shape qualities.
   In each case, in the diagram, the horizontal cross is considered the substrate of the other elements.

3. Elements which occupy similar positions
   in each diagram are considered affinities. This means that the effort element is most easily performed with the
   corresponding shape element, in theory.
   The affinities are as follows: lightness with rising; strength with sinking;
   indirectness with spreading; directness
   with enclosing; slowness with advancing;
   suddenness with retreating. The affinities do not, by any means, always appear together in movement but are considered by some to be most naturally
   performed together.

SUPPLEMENTARY
CONCEPTS

- SPATIAL ORIENTATION
- BODY PART INVOLVEMENT IN MOVEMENT
- BODY ATTITUDE

SUPPLEMENTARY
CONCEPTS

SPATIAL ORIENTATION

The differentiation and labelling of directions in space is implicit in the notation and terminology of both directional and shaping movement and also in Dr. Kestenberg's more specific notation for shape flow. However, there may be occasions in observing movement when you want to consider which directions in space are used apart from the spatial form of the movement. For example, in a dance, you may want to ask what are the predominant directions the dancer moves in, apart from whether the dancer shapes or moves directionally. Even if you do use the various directions only within the context of the shape categories, it is helpful to have a way of naming places in space and of recognizing them in movement. This orientation, as it is presented here, is a part of Laban's theoretical work important in both Labanotation and Effort/Shape.

The upright human being has a three-dimensional orientation to space. This means
he has access to the height, width and
depth of the surrounding space. The limits
of an individual's reach into space without
changing place, or taking a step, Laban
called the kinesphere. Directions or areas
within the kinesphere can be distinguished
and labelled, and the naming process is
accomplished through the orientation of
the three-dimensional cross of axes.

When an individual is upright, the longi-
tudinal axis of his body, the body midline,
coincides with the plumb-line of the pull
of gravity through his body toward the
center of the earth. This line we call
the vertical dimension, or axis, which is
composed of the two directions, up, away
from the pull of gravity, and down, toward
the pull of gravity. Two other axes inter-
sect the vertical axis at right angles, so
that all three axes are equidistant - the
horizontal axis going from side to side,
and the sagittal axis going forward and
backward.

The description of directions in space by
the six directions in the dimensional cross
of axes appears to be a convention based
on our uprightness, and to a certain extent,
on the fact that our locomotion patterns,
our buildings and furnishings (walls, doors,
tables, chairs, etc.) are based on this
vertical-horizontal-sagittal grid. If our
structures were more similar to that of the
chambered nautilus, or if we shaped our environment more according to crystalline
forms such as the geodesic dome, we would
undoubtedly define space using a different
kind of emphasis.

You can describe where movement goes in the kinesphere by means of these six directions, which are called the six spatial tendencies, or by combinations of two or three of these spatial tendencies. In the Labanotation symbols which denote all of these directions, directions upward and downward are included within the concept of level - high, middle, low - and movement coinciding with the vertical midline is termed "place."

(See illustration on page 71)

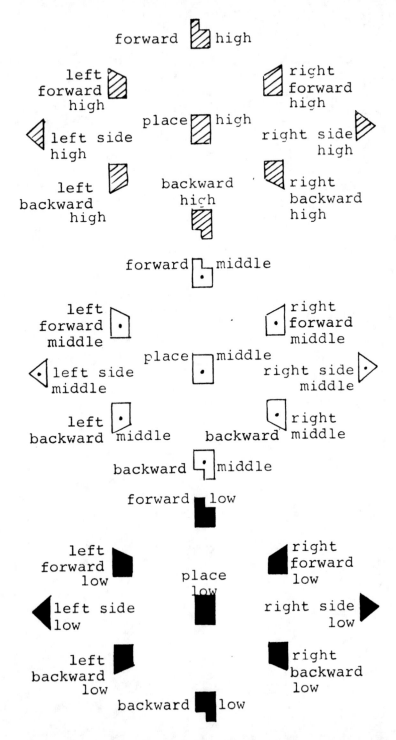

The above directions are seen in terms of the upright body with a constant "front," i.e., with (usually) the pelvis remaining forward throughout. Directions named by a single spatial tendency - high, low, (up, down), right side, left side, forward, backward, are sometimes called dimensional because they constitute the three-dimensional cross of axes. Directions named by two or three spatial tendencies, such as forward-high or right-backward-low, are generally referred to as diagonal, although there are more specific ways of differentiating among them. If you choose to make use of direction names apart from the concepts of directional and shaping movement, remember that movement involving any specific direction can be done a number of ways, i.e., with a number of possible forms. For example, if a movement involves the

direction right-forward-high, ▨ which combines three spatial tendencies, it does not necessarily involve a three-dimensional movement form, i.e., shaping. You can point right-forward-high in a directional spoke-like way, or in a directional arc-like way, or you can shape yourself into the direction right-forward-high by spreading advancing, rising.

Many basic body movements combine two spatial tendencies, so that it is often appropriate in movement to describe space not only in terms of points or tendencies radiating from the center of the cross of axes, but also in terms of planes or cycles which combine two dimensions. Walking, running, turning, cartwheeling, somersaulting, all occur in what can be called cycles or planes.

Although any flat, cyclic movement can describe a plane, the concept of plane
evolves from the cross of axes. Thus,
when we speak of planes or cycles, we speak
of only three: the vertical cycle (door
plane, cartwheel cycle) which combines the
dimensions up-down and side-side and has
as its axis the forward-backward dimension;
the horizontal cycle (table plane, turning
cycle) which combines the dimensions side-
side and forward-backward and has as its
axis the upward-downward or vertical dimension; the sagittal cycle (wheel plane,
somersault cycle) which combines the dimensions forward-backward and up-down and has
as its axis the side open-side across (right-
left) or horizontal dimension.

Our skeletal and muscular systems, or our
perception of them reflect this concept of
three planes based on the cross of axes.
The body is divided by the horizontal plane
into upper and lower, by the vertical plane
into frontal and dorsal, and by the sagittal
plane into right and left halves. The anatomical analysis of joint movement also
uses this concept of planes or cycles. We
can speak of flexion-extension as producing
movement in the sagittal cycle primarily,
of abduction and adduction as mainly vertical cycle movement, and inward and out-
ward rotation as facilitating movement in
the horizontal cycle.

When the mover is lying on the floor, and
you want to refer to a direction, a problem arises, since the body midline no
longer coincides with the vertical axis of
space or the kinesphere. One convention
you can use in this case is to speak of

directions in terms of the body orientation,
i.e., headward, feetward, or of the room
orientation, i.e., ceilingward, toward the
floor; or you may want to use a combination
of both.

For a more detailed understanding of spatial orientation in movement, you are referred to Laban's theories of Space Harmony
or Choreutics, and to the spatial concepts
included in Labanotation, especially the
concepts of Crosses of Axes.

S U P P L E M E N T A R Y   C O N C E P T S

BODY PART INVOLVEMENT IN MOVEMENT

When Laban developed the concepts which
eventually led to Effort/Shape, he was
concentrating on what might be called the
high points of man's movement life - the
activities in which man was called upon to
crystallize his attitude, his intent, his
action - such as dance and theater movement,
fencing, fighting, skilled physical work.
Thus, the Effort/Shape terms, for the most
part, reflect these crystallized movement.

Application of Effort/Shape in this country,
however, led to areas in which the movement
life is not so consistently at a high level
of crystallization - areas like child development, physical rehabilitation, family
therapy research and dance therapy for
hospitalized patients, as well as basic
movement teaching and correctives work.
Thus, although strength and lightness, for
example, are the crystallized qualities

produced with an active attitude toward
the weight, there are contexts in which
such an attitude toward weight may be an
unfamiliar experience for movers, or might
be seen only partially, as in the child's
learning process. In such cases less crystallized movement phenomena related to the
active qualities must be sought, whether
by teacher or observer.

For situations such as these which appeared
in the studio and research projects, a number of supplementary concepts relating to
the body began to be added to Effort theory.
In a sense, this was a process of "building
down" from the level of Effort/Shape description relevant for highly active, high-
involvement situations. Dr. Kestenberg
found that she could find many of the terms
she needed by a more detailed examination
of effort flow and shape flow, while a
number of other people fell heir to the
extensive physical therapy experience of
Irmgard Bartenieff and from her began to
understand the relationship of anatomical
and body-level description to the Effort
theory.

The following concepts relating to body
part involvement in the movement can be
seen as "ingredients" of various Effort
and Shape elements, necessary for but not
equal to the elements themselves.

To denote which part of the body is involved in a movement, we use the body
part symbols from Labanotation:

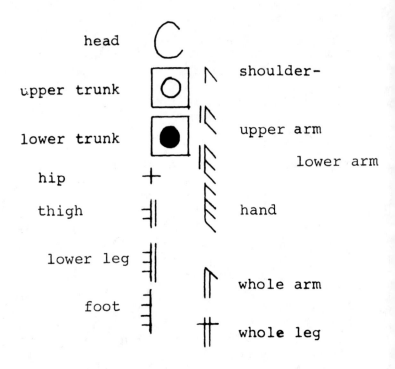

You can speak of a body part <u>initiating</u> a movement, <u>being active</u> in a movement but not necessarily initiating it, or <u>consistently leading</u> a movement, as in the idea of trace form. Sometimes you may want to say that a part is <u>actively held</u>, such as in a Charlie Chaplin walk, where the feet and legs are held and moved against a held trunk.

Any part of the body may produce a movement possessing any Effort or Shape quality. However, there is a tendency to associate strength with activation of the lower unit (pelvis and legs), and lightness with activation of the upper unit (upper trunk

and arms), where the lower serves a supporting function. The pelvis is sometimes
called the center of weight or center of
gravity, the chest the center of levity.

The body parts may also be grouped in terms
of those closest to the center - upper and
lower trunk, sometimes including shoulder
and hip joints - and those on the periphery -
head, lower arms and hands, lower legs and
feet. You can speak of a movement as centrally initiated and/or active or peripher-
ally initiated and/or active. Rock and
roll dancing is mainly a centrally initiated activity, crocheting a peripheral one.*
Lightness, associated as it is with a quality of touch, may often be readily evoked
using peripheral movement, while central
movement lends itself best to strength.

Another way of grouping the body parts in
movement description is in terms of one or
both sides of the body. Movement which involves both sides equally affording a balance of activity on both sides may be
termed bilateral. Movement initiated by
or emphasizing one body side is called
unilateral. In swimming, the breaststroke

*In Laban's Choreutics or Space Harmony,
central refers to a pathway in space which
passes through the center of the body,
while peripheral refers to movement that
remains at the outer edges of the kinesphere, i.e., in far reach space, on the
periphery of the sphere of reach. This is
a specialized use of central and peripheral concerned with the body in a specific
relationship to space.

is bilateral, the crawl unilateral in each
stroke. As you will readily agree if you
try reaching for something bilaterally,
then unilaterally, the latter tends to
lead you into adaptation in space and into
locomotion, whereas bilateral movement is
more likely to emphasize stability.

The terms simultaneous and sequential or
successive refer to the inclusion of body
parts in movement either all at once, simultaneously, or in a wave-like sequence,
where the movement spreads through adjacent
parts successively. A belly-dancer is
likely to move successively, while a swim-
mer doing a racing dive will probably be
simultaneous in his movement. Sequential
or successive inclusion of body parts is
often an ingredient of the effort element
indirectness, and less consistently of
shaping.

Finally, a most important aspect of body
part involvement is how much of the body
is involved in the movement. To describe
this, Warren Lamb coined the terms posture
and gesture. When any movement activates
the whole body to a noticeable extent it
is called postural. The movement may involve primarily a single body part, but if
the whole body reflects the movement, even
if it is an emphatic shake of the head
which is actively supported through the
body, it is a postural movement - in this
case a postural movement of the head. When
movement activates only a part of the body
it is called gestural.*

*Certain practitioners, notably Warren

Postural movement is closely associated with trunk movement, and especially with shifts of weight, although on rare occasions you may see isolated gestures of the trunk, or even gestural walking. It is safe to say, however, that weight shift and locomotion in movement is usually postural. A certain proportion of all movement is postural, and studies have shown that the proportion increases with the involvement of the mover in his experience.* You may have seen conversations which gradually turned into arguments. If you were out of hearing range, you would still be likely to understand the way things were going by the fact of the movers' becoming more and more involved in their interaction - literally so, with more and more of the body participating· more of the time. Such a situation would illustrate an increasing proportion of postural movement. Or you may have watched, with some distrust, a speaker who restricted himself mainly to gestural movement, yet repeatedly assured

---

Lamb, use the term postural only when movement throughout the total body is consistent, i.e, when the whole body is participating in the same Effort or Shape quality. For example, Lamb would not consider postural a movement of the whole body in which one part was rising, another enclosing.

*See Martha Davis, A Study and Experiment in Expressive Movement, 1965, unpublished manuscript available at the Dance Notation Bureau.

his audience of his involvement in his
topic.

NOTATION

The categories of posture and gesture are
part of Effort/Shape notation. A postural
movement is signified by the letter P, with
a body part symbol following if it initi-
ates in a particular part. For example,
an excited wave of the right arm involving

the whole body would be notated as P $\mathsf{\Uparrow}$.
A gestural movement is signified by the
symbol for the gesturing body part; it is
assumed to be gestural if no "P" precedes
it.

SUPPLEMENTARY CONCEPTS

BODY ATTITUDE

So far the concepts presented for use in movement observation have shared one common feature: they all describe something about the qualitative changes in the <u>ongoing movement process</u>. The concept of body attitude is of a slightly different nature; it is concerned with what qualities are <u>maintained</u> in the body, which spatial emphases, body part relationships and tensions are held in the body as a kind of baseline from which the mover operates.

People in various disciplines have selected different phenomena to investigate as part of body attitude, according to their particular needs. Some of these are covered below, although there are undoubtedly many other possibilities to investigate.

USE OF TRUNK:

Looking at the relationship within the trunk itself has been an important distinguishing feature in cross-cultural studies. It is probably less useful in studies within a single culture, since the use of the trunk seems to distinguish cultures more than individuals within one culture. The following ways of defining the use of the trunk are either adapted from or taken directly from various Choreometrics* coding sheets:

1) As a solid unit: where the trunk articulates as one piece. You might see this in dances where the trunk is held, such as Scottish or 15th century court dances.

2) As divided right and left by the midline: a person might be said to have this body attitude who transfers the weight in stepping from side to side rather than along a central path.

3) As two units, upper and lower: where there is separate and opposing articulation of upper and lower trunk, as in well done versions of such popular dances as the twist and frug.

4) As four quadrants, right and left upper and right and left lower: allowing for the diagonal relationship

*See Lomax, op.cit. and CORD, op.cit.

of the upper quadrant with the opposite-side lower quadrant. An approximation of this might be seen in the walk of a fashion model, or in some Graham-derivative modern dance styles.

SPATIAL STRESS:

The concept of spatial stress as a way of describing body attitude does not refer so much to the space outside the individual as it does to his "inner space," his feeling of his own length, width, and depth in relationship to the environment. Spatial stress may be a valuable category for studies within a culture, and has already proved valuable for cross-cultural study. The following variations of spatial stress are taken directly from Choreometrics coding sheets:

1) Neutral erect: where the head-neck-trunk remains fairly fixed around the vertical midline of the body, without particular stress on the length or verticality of the body.

2) Vertical erect: in which the body length is stressed, the feeling of uprightness and verticality maintained.

3) Horizontal stress: where the body width is emphasized, including width in the stance; spreading in the horizontal dimension.

4) Sagittal stress: in which the feeling of uprightness is combined with the use of the trunk in a shoulder-opposite-hip relationship.

BODY PARTS HELD OR INERT:

For some purposes, it may be useful to look
at body attitude in terms of what body
parts are held or inert. It is important
in movement teaching, especially on a cor-
rective level, and has been found useful
in observing actors' movement. These more
detailed observations affect the total
picture of the configuration of trunk and
limbs which characterizes a person. Often
it is the major clue in the "something
about" a person which allows you to recognize him at a distance. Whether a body
part is held or inert, it prohibits movement from passing through it. Dr. Kesten-
bert uses the alternative terms "tension
spot" for a part held and "dead spot" for
an inert place in the body. That such
"spots" are often found close together or
related is important only for correctives
work. More generally, you may want to note
that a person's shoulders are held, or that
the center of weight seems relatively inert.

TOTAL BODY SHAPES:

Sometimes body attitude may appear as a
constantly held shape of the total body or
a large part of the body such as upper or
lower unit. If it is convenient to describe body attitude in terms of total body
shape, terms like concave, convex, rounded,
flat, twisted may be used. If large por-
tions of the body maintain a constant shape,
you may want to adapt the shape flow terms
to describe them, such as closed in the
upper, opened in the lower, closed on one
side, etc.

The concept of body attitude is quite generalized and complex in comparison with most Effort/Shape concepts. It is concerned with a larger configuration of phenomena, and therefore the ways in which it can be regarded are as varied as the needs of the observer. A description of body attitude may involve one or several of the concepts of use of the trunk, spatial stress, parts held or inert, total shape or opened-closed relationships of large body units.

Dr. Kestenberg is an example of someone who combines many concepts in her use of body attitude. She uses the terms "tension line" and "shape," which involve in part or in toto all of the following categories: 1) parts held, active or inert; 2) parts in relation to each other; 3) relation to reach space and spatial stress; 4) the quality and intensity of flow; 5) the spread of movement through the body (inclusion of parts). Her approach demonstrates how inclusive the concept of body attitude can be. Choreometrics research stresses in the concept of body attitude the use of the trunk and spatial stress, noting other characteristics in other categories.

Body attidute is sometimes used to gain an over-all picture of a.person's movement tendencies. For instance, based on the theoretical affinities between effort and shape elements, a body attitude with vertical stress might produce a movement repertoire with a large proportion of up-down movement with its effort affinities of lightness and strength. But it must be stressed that evidence for such predictions based on body attitude is not at all con- clusive at this point.

PATTERNS OF MOVEMENT

PATTERNS OF MOVEMENT

The approach you find most useful for looking at movement in patterns will depend on
the context in which you research or teach
or direct or perform movement. At the
present time, there are a variety of such
contexts involving a variety of people and
disciplines. Some people, such as Dr. Kestenberg and Warren Lamb, are involved in
assessment of movement repertoires. This
means that they notate in detail many movement sequences performed by an individual,
perhaps in several situations. Then they
perform statistical operations from their
data to arrive at movement profiles of individuals. Other people work in contexts
which combine assessing with teaching their
subjects. Sometimes this occurs in a hos-
pital situation where patients are observed
and then taught, in dance therapy sessions,
perhaps in consultation with a psychother-
apist. Research projects such as Choreometrics and the work of anthropologist
Allison Jablonko involve assessing not one
but many people belonging to a similar
ethnic group. Parameters for looking at

groups must differ from those for describing individuals. And some people use Effort/Shape in the studio alone, where information about movement sequences is absorbed by the teacher and modified and fed back without intervening notation or statistics.

Whatever the context within which you must organize your information, one or several of the following five methods of organization will be helpful. Their presentation here is quite sketchy, but each is a method of describing patterns of the appearance of Effort/Shape elements in movement. The five are: 1) combinations of movement elements; 2) proportions of frequency of use among elements; 3) the emphasized movement elements; 4) the range of elements used; 5) the sequence or phrasing of movement elements.

COMBINATION - WHAT APPEARS WITH WHAT

Any effort and shape elements can appear together simultaneously except those which are by definition mutually exclusive. All opposite effort elements (free-bound, light-strong, etc.) and shape flow-directional-shaping are mutually exclusive in any moving unit of the body at any one time. If you are looking at the continuous changes in any one element, such as strength in the figure of Death in The Green Table, discussed above, what that element combines with will be an important consideration.

A great deal of theoretical work has been done on the significance of different effort combinations, first by Laban (in Mastery of Movement) and later by Marion North. Laban's Choreutics is a complex study of the significance of combining various spatial tendencies in different sequences with effort.

PROPORTION - WHAT APPEARS HOW MUCH MORE OR LESS THAT WHAT

When an observer looks for the frequency with which each element appears in movement, and compares the frequencies of the Effort Shape elements in an individual's repertoire, the result can be diagrammed in a movement profile, a graphic picture of the proportions of each element to the others. Warren Lamb originated the movement profile for his work in aptitude assessment. Dr. Kestenberg also uses the profile method in her developmental studies of children.

EMPHASIS - WHAT SEEMS TO BE STRESSED

Very often, especially in studio work or in the theater, the observer, whether director, dancer, critic, must rely on a general, overall impression of the movement pattern to make sense of it. He must ask, "What is the main statement? What is the theme? What strikes me about it?" In effect, he is asking what elements are emphasized in the total pattern.

In the famous eating scene from the film Tom Jones, for example, the theme is expressed in the interaction between the couple in the implications of their various approaches to their food. The main emphasis of the scene is on the indirect or direct approach to the food, and, by implication, to the other person, with additional variation from the time factor and occasionally from strength.

This way of looking at patterns can be quite subjective; it can also be quite accurate.

RANGE - HOW WHAT ACTUALLY APPEARS RELATES TO WHAT IS POSSIBLE

In observing the range of the movement repertoire, the actual number of elements used (and the frequency of their use) is compared with the standard of the full range of possible use of the elements. Observation of an individual's range allows the observer to see what the mover has in his repertoire and what he lacks.

SEQUENCE OR PHRASING - WHAT FOLLOWS WHAT

Research involving detailed analysis of phrasing in Effort-Shape is minimal* in part because of the complexity of studying phrases. The need for more understanding of phrasing is apparent, especially in such areas as acting and the study of small-group interaction.

---

*See Martha Davis, Methods for Perceiving Patterns in Small Group Behavior. New York, Dance Notation Bureau Press, 1977.

The most that can be offered here with regard to phrasing is a few guidelines for
looking at movement in sequences. Movement
is not always, at every moment, making its
main statement; it has an exertion-recuper-
ation rhythm that creates the phrase. Even
everyday movement tends to organize itself
into phrases that somehow initiate, make
their main statement, and conclude, the
conslusion often being a transition into
another phrase. Here, then are four orientation questions: 1) how does the phrase
initiate or prepare for the main statement?
2) where is the main statement or emphasis?
(beginning, middle, end, toward the begin-
ing, toward the end, etc.) 3) how is the
phrase concluded? 4) how is the transition
made to the next phrase?

A helpful way to capture the sequence of
the phrase is by reproducing it in another
medium - either drawing a representation
of the rhythm and shape of the sequence,
or "singing" the sequence. The windup and
throwing of a ball might be drawn:

or might be sung: mmmmmmmmmmmmmmmmmmmmmmbah

Another characteristic to look for in
phrasing is its degree of liveliness, fluctuation, changeability, or its evenness,
creating a monotone. These two contrasting
characteristics might be related to whether
or not the mover makes use of real recuper-
ation and renewal in movement, using effort
and shape flow to build up to something, or
changing into contrasting kinds of concentration, or using an upbeat or rebound of

an opposite effort element, such as lightness, to produce a main statement, such as
strength.

It sometimes very important to note the
type of transition a mover makes from one
phrase to the next. Types of spatial
transition were mentioned in Part II; the
concept of effort transition is touched
upon in the appendix in the discussion of
procedures for notating phrases. Postural
movement is often important in making
transitions.

Martha Davis* has compared movement phrases
described with Effort/Shape to the melodies,
rhythms, themes of music. If you listen
to the "music" of a conversation, without
paying attention to the verbal content, you
will experience something similar to the
"dance" of the non-verbal part of a conversation, a series of rhythmic, related or-
ganizations of movement qualities.

---

*Ibid.

APPENDICES

A P P E N D I X I

PROCEDURE FOR NOTATING MOVEMENT

PHRASES WITH EFFORT SHAPE

The following is a sample movement phrase
recorded with effort/shape notation. It
gives a visual idea of how the notation
looks in its final form. The steps and
rules for notating such phrases are then
enumerated.

(a postural movement of the right forearm
beginning free-quick rising and spreading
with bound lightness followed by 5 gestures sinking strong rising free then ending with quick bound advancing and sinking
to closing while still sinking in **exaggerated** bound flow.)

1. Record <u>movement change</u> in any part of the body.

2. <u>Gesture</u> - <u>Posture</u>

   First note whether the movement is gestural or postural. If it is a postural sequence write P; if it is gestural begin the notation with the body part. A movement phrase is assumed to be gestural unless "P" is written.

   $\mathsf{P}\mathsf{E}$. . . . . postural movement

   $\mathsf{3}\mathsf{E}$. . . . . gestural movement of both forearms

   Note: While P indicates that the movement involves the whole body, the predominant body part active in the postural movement may be noted (see for ex. above). An example of this might be a handshake, where the arm-hand is the predominant part involved in the postural movement.

3. Body Part

   Record the body part or parts actively involved in the movement, noting the largest unit moving according to the symbols taken from Labanotation. The body part symbols, written one above the other, indicate these parts move simultaneously.

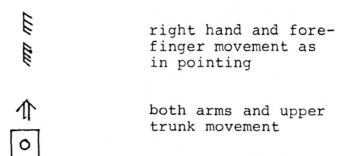

right hand and fore-
finger movement as
in pointing

both arms and upper
trunk movement

4.   Notation Order

Effort and shape symbols are written
from left to right, the effort symbols above the shape. Effort and
shape elements which occur simultaneously are written one directly above
the other.

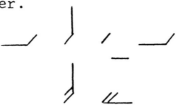

Note: In this example indirect and

widening occur together ⌡ as do quick

and closing.

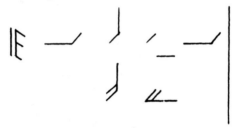

5. Start and End of Phrase

In phrase recording movement is described from perceptible start to
stop. The beginning is indicated by
P or body part and the end of the
phrase by a bar.

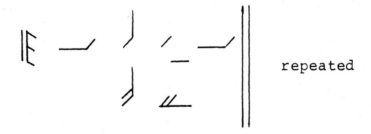

6. Repetition

    a.   If the entire phrase is repeated
without a stop write a double bar
at the end. If it is repeated
more than twice write a double bar
and the number of times repeated.

repeated

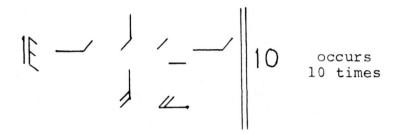

occurs
10 times

b. If a part of the phrase is repeated, enclose the part repeated
   in the dots   , write the number
   of times repeated and finish the
   phrase.

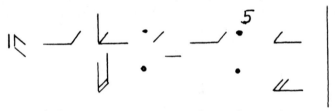

(The movement begins free becomes
light and bound as it rises and
widens, followed by 5 movements
quick to free, the phrase ending
in bound closing.)

7. Sustained elements:

Only changes in movement are recorded
in effort shape.   If the notation goes
from one element or combination of

elements to another (eg. ⌐ ⌐), the

notation indicates the effort or shape
elements changed from one to another
(eg. changed from slow indirect bound

to quick strong), i.e. the first elements "disappear" and are followed by
new dynamics. It is possible, however,
that an element or several elements
may continue while the movement
changes. If an effort or shape element is sustained through a sequence
this is indicated by a sustain sign:

Any effort or shape quality or flow
may be sustained except quickness.

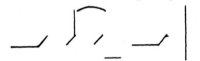

the indirectness is maintained as
the movement becomes quick

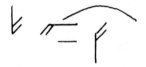

the enclosure continues from the
enclosing retreating action into
the sinking.

Note: the sustaining bar ⌒ goes
from the tip of the symbol being sustained into the "place" it would have

in the next symbol, eg. ⌡ ⌐ . If
two elements are sustained, two bars

are required, eg. ⌡⌐

8.   Succession

Movement may spread from one body part
to another or from postures to gestures

and vice versa. If the succession is
uninterrupted but distinctly separate
it is noted. Also an effort or shape
element which occurs in one part and
spreads into another part is not noted
as a new effort or shape, but as the
sustaining of an effort or shape to a
new body part. For there to be succession of an effort or shape to another body part the body part must be
connected to the first.

a widening retreating of the head
in which the widening continues in
the shoulder

sinking in the arms followed by
sinking in the trunk

If a movement **phrase** goes from postural movement to gestures or vice versa,
it is written so:

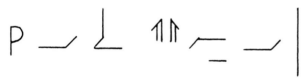

a postural movement which becomes
a gesture of both arms

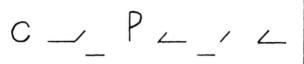

a head gesture which becomes
postural

If a postural movement occurs and is
followed by movement predominantly in
one part but still postural, it is
written:

i.e. total body movement becoming a
movement predominantly of the right
arm although the whole phrase is
postural.

Note: if the body parts in a continuous movement are not connected (ana-
tomically) but the same effort or
shape elements occurs first in one
part then in the ohter, this would be
a new occurence of the element. That
is, the element does not spread from
one part to another but is "recreated"
in the separate part.

a continuous movement: the right
arm widening followed by widening
in the left arm.

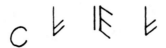

the head rising followed by rising
in the forearm.

9. Holds

Within a phrase the movement may per-
ceptibly pause or be held. If an
effort is sustained through this pause,
this is not considered the end of the
movement phrase but a hold within it.
The hold is indicated by a °

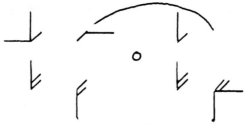

the movement pauses while the directness is maintained into the second
rising.

Note: in very exact notation this may
be used to indicate one part moves
then is held while another continues.

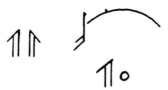

both arms widen, then one arm is
held as the other continues to widen

10. Body Parts having different dynamics

Frequently movement in one part of
the body is different from movement
occuring at the same time in another
part. This requires separate lines
of notation, one for each part. Again
dynamics which occur together should
be written one directly under the
other.

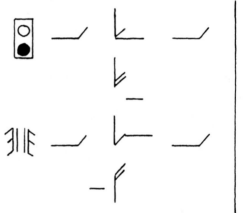

the trunk rises and retreats with
bound lightness as the forearms
advance and sink with direct lightness

11. Upbeat and Rebound

Rebound: often, particularly in repetitive two-phase movements, the
first phase is accented or emphasized
while the second phase is a rebound
toward the opposite dynamics eg ⌐to⌐ .

The "rebound" from the main dynamic is
not as active producing of a new
effort or shape but goes toward the

opposite of the emphasized effort or
shape.

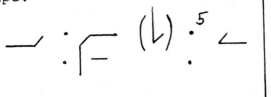

this might be a hammering movement
beginning free followed by 5 movements strong-quick direct with a
rebound into lightness ending in
bound flow.

Note: as the example indicated, the
rebound may be the reverse of one of
the dynamics or it may be a combination. It is always one action indicated by (   ).

Upbeat: similar to the rebound, there
may be at the start of a movement a
slight preparation or upbeat before
going into the main action. The upbeat is always the opposite effort or
shape dynamic of the main dynamics.

an upbeat of rising before advancing
and sinking then closing

Note: An upbeat refers to the beginning of a phrase, rebound refers to a
phrase that may follow an effort or
shape element. Both are single actions
indicated by (   ).

12. "Crescendoes"

If an effort or shape becomes increasingly or decreasingly emphasized in a phrase, especially in repetitive movement this may be noted with

< (increasing) or > (decreasing)

symbols. The element which is gradually increased or decreased is written with these symbols.

a hand movement which in the repeated phases (quick to free) becomes increasingly quicker.

Another example which may be visualized is a circular movement which becomes increasingly quicker and quicker.

A P P E N D I X   I I

COMBINATIONS OF THREE EFFORT ELEMENTS

The four effort factors can be combined in groups of three in four groups: Time-Space-Weight; Time-Space-Flow; Time-Weight-Flow; Space-Weight-Flow. Since each factor has two elements, each group yields eight different combinations of three elements.

The eight combinations of three elements in a group can be performed in a sequence in which only one element is changed from one combination to the next. Beginning with the most "indulging" combination of three, you can go through a sequence of seven changes to arrive at the most "fighting" combination, changing the quality of only one factor at a time. There are six different sequences of change which meet these requirements in each group.

ci = change in

WEIGHT - SPACE - TIME (W-S-T)

Weight, space and time factors in combination are termed effort actions or full efforts. They require utmost concentration and full activation of the body weight, oriented in space and time. So action oriented are these eight full efforts that Laban attached an everyday action word to each of them.

FLOAT   WRING   PRESS   GLIDE
indirect   indirect   direct   direct
light   strong   strong   light
sustained   sustained   sustained   sustained
(indulging)

DAB   FLICK   SLASH   PUNCH
direct   indirect   indirect   direct
light   light   strong   strong
quick   quick   quick   quick
                                             (fighting)

Here the sequence of change is W-S-W-T-S-W-S, where the time quality is maintained on either side of the middle change. The other five possible sequences for weight-space-time are:
1. S-W-S-T-W-S-W, the reverse of the above
2. T-S-T-W-S-T-S, where the weight quality is maintained until the middle

3. S-T-S-W-T-S-T, the reverse of #2
4. W-T-W-S-T-W-T, where the space quality is maintained until the middle
5. T-W-T-S-W-T-W, the reverse of #4

WEIGHT - FLOW - TIME (W-F-T)

c_i = change in

light	strong	strong	light
free	free	free	free
sustained.	sustained	quick	quick
(indulging)			

light	light	strong	strong
bound	bound	bound	bound
quick	sustained	sustained	quick
			(fighting)

Here the sequence of change is W-T-W-F-T-W-T, where the same flow quality is maintained on either side of the middle change. The other five possible sequences which may begin with indulging and end with full fighting combinations, changing only one quality at a time are:
1. T-W-T-F-W-T-W, the reverse of the above
2. F-T-F-W-T-F-T, where weight quality remains the same on either side of the middle

3. T-F-T-W-F-T-F, the reverse of #2
4. F-W-F-T-W-F-W, where time remains the
    same on either side of the middle
5. W-F-W-T-F-W-F, the reverse of #4

SPACE - WEIGHT - FLOW (S-W-F)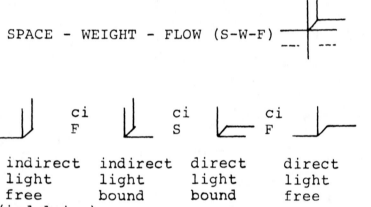

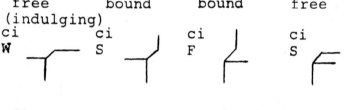

Here the sequence of change is F-S-F-W-S-F-S, where the same weight quality is maintained on either side of the middle. The five other possible sequences are:
1. S-F-S-W-F-S-F, the reverse of the above
2. W-S-W-F-S-W-S, where the flow quality remains the same until the middle
3. S-W-S-F-W-S-W, the reverse of #2
4. W-F-W-S-F-W-F, where the space quality remains the same until the middle

5. F-W-F-S-W-F-W, the reverse of #4

TIME - SPACE - FLOW (T-S-F)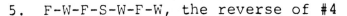

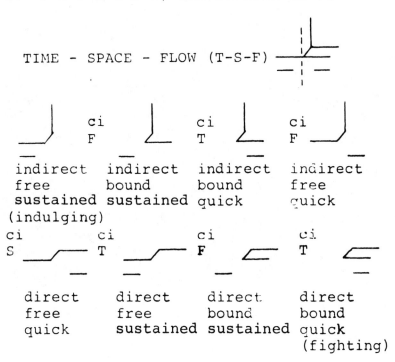

| | ci F | | ci T | | ci F | | ci |
| indirect free sustained (indulging) | indirect bound sustained | | indirect bound quick | | indirect free quick | |

| ci S | | ci T | | ci F | | ci T | |
| direct free quick | direct free sustained | | direct bound sustained | | direct bound quick (fighting) | |

Here the sequence of change is F-T-F-S-T-F-T, where space is maintained in quality until the middle change. The five other possible sequences are:
1. T-F-T-S-F-T-F, the reverse of the above
2. S-T-S-F-T-S-T, where flow quality is maintained until the middle
3. T-S-T-F-S-T-S, the reverse of #2
4. S-F-S-T-F-S-F, where time quality is maintained until the middle
5. F-S-F-T-S-F-S, the reverse of #4

COMBINATIONS OF TWO EFFORT ELEMENTS

The four effort factors can be combined
in two's in six groups: space-time;
weight-flow; weight-time; space-flow;
flow-time; space-weight.   These six
groups can be seen as three pairs of
opposites.   Since each factor has two
elements, each group yields four possible
combinations of two elements.

(See illustrations on following pages)

SPACE & TIME
(AWAKE)

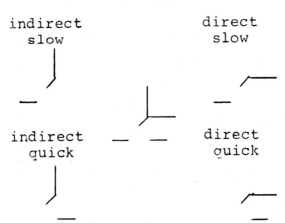

indirect
slow

direct
slow

indirect
quick

direct
quick

WEIGHT & TIME
(NEAR RHYTHM)

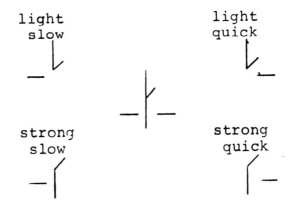

light
slow

light
quick

strong
slow

strong
quick

WEIGHT & FLOW
(DREAM)

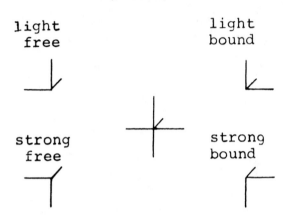

light
free

light
bound

strong
free

strong
bound

SPACE & FLOW
(REMOTE)

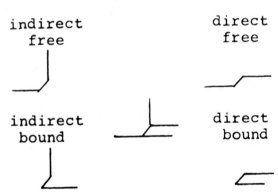

indirect
free

direct
free

indirect
bound

direct
bound

FLOW & TIME
(MOBILE)

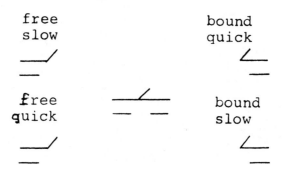

free
slow

bound
quick

free
quick

bound
slow

SPACE & WEIGHT
(STABILE)

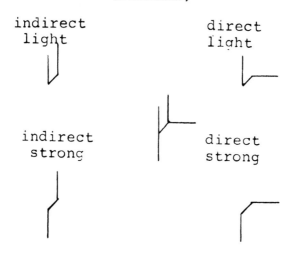

indirect
light

direct
light

indirect
strong

direct
strong

A P P E N D I X   I I I

NOTATION OF SHAPE FLOW –

SYMMETRICAL AND ASYMMETRICAL

Dr. Kestenberg, in her research with
young children, has found a need to distinguish not only the expansion-contrac-
tion aspect of shape flow, but also, more
specifically, in which dimension the shape
flow occurs. She regards this more specific description of shape flow as a kind
of step toward directional movement, just
as the attributes of tension flow are
precursors of more specific effort elements. Dr. Kestenberg has evolved two
sets of symbols based on the symbols for
growing and shrinking above. All of these
symbols denote shape flow; one set covers
the variations in symmetrical shape flow,
the other in asymmetrical shape flow.

SYMMETRICAL SHAPE FLOW:

The symbols for symmetrical shape flow
follow. In each of the six cases, the
opposing body halves - whether upper and

lower, right and left sides, or front and back - both do the same thing, e.g., if the front bulges forward, the back bulges backward.

~———⫽   -growing, spreading to sides

├——⫽   -growing, lengthening up and down

/——⫽   -growing, bulging forward and
         backward

⫽——~   -shrinking, enclosing

⫽——┤   -shrinking, shortening upper and
         lower toward center

⫽——/   -shrinking, hollowing or thinning
         back and front toward center

ASYMMETRICAL SHAPE FLOW

The symbols for asymmetrical shape flow follow. Here, in each case, only one of the opposing body halves does the growing and shrinking, while the other half may make a passive adjustment to the movement; e.g., if the front of the body hollows, the result in the back of the body will be convexity, or a passive bulging backward.

←⫽ - growing to one side

└⫽ -growing, lengthening upward

┌⫽ -growing, lengthening, downward

└⫽ -growing, bulging forward

┌⫽ -growing, bulging backward

⟋⟶ -shrinking one side toward center

⟋⌐ -shrinking, shortening upward

⟋⌐ -shrinking, shortening downward

⟋⟋ -shrinking, hollowing forward

⟋⌐ -shrinking, hollowing backward

BIBLIOGRAPHY

Bartenieff, Irmgard. <u>Effort-Shape in Relation to Anatomy and Neurophysiology</u>. Lecture to be published by Dance Notation Bureau, summer, 1970.

_____. <u>Laban Theory as an Aesthetic Formulation</u>. Lecture to be published by Dance Notation Bureau, summer, 1970.

_____. <u>Notes from a Course in Correctives</u>. To be published by the Dance Notation Bureau, summer, 1970

_____. "Research in Anthropology: A Study of Dance in Primitive Cultures" in <u>The Proceedings of the Preliminary Conference on Research in Dance</u>. New York, Committee on Research in Dance, 1967.

Bartenieff, Irmgard, and Davis, Martha. <u>Effort-Shape Analysis of Movement: The Unity of Function and Expression</u>. New York, Albert Einstein College of Medicine, 1965.

Bartenieff, Irmgard, Lomax, Alan, and Paulay, Forrestine. Chapters X, XI, XII, in <u>Folk Song Style and Culture</u>. Washington, American Association for the Advancement of Science, 1968.

Davis, Martha. <u>A Study and Experiment in Expressive Movement</u>. Unpublished manuscript, New York University, 1964.

Davis, Martha. <u>Methods of Perceiving Patterns in Small Group Behavior</u>. New York, Dance Notation Bureau Press, 1977.

Davis, Martha and Schmais, Claire. "An Analysis of the Style and Composition of <u>Water Study</u>" in the <u>Proceedings of the Preliminary Conference on Research in Dance</u>. New York, Committee on Research in Dance. 1967.

Kestenberg, Judith. "The Role of Movement Patterns in Development: I. Rhythms of Movement" in <u>Psychoanalytic Quarterly</u>, Vol. XXXIV, No. 1, 1965.

_____. "The Role of Movement Patterns in Development: II. The Flow of Tension and Effort" in <u>Psychoanalytic Quarterly</u>, Vol. XXXIV, No. 4, 1965.

_____. "The Role of Movement Patterns in Development: III. The Control of Shape" in <u>Psychoanalytic Quarterly</u>, Vol. XXXVI, No. 3, 1967.

Laban, Rudolf. <u>Choreutics</u>. London, Macdonald and Evans, 1966

_____. <u>The Mastery of Movement</u>. London, Macdonald and Evans, 1960, (2nd edition revised by Lisa Ullmann)

_____. <u>Modern Educational Dance</u>. London, Macdonald and Evans, 1948, (2nd edition revised by Lisa Ullmann)

_____. <u>Principles of Dance and</u>

Movement Notation. London, Macdonald
    and Evans, 1956.

Laban, Rudolf, and Lawrence, F.C.   Effort.
    London, Macdonald and Evans. 1947.

Lamb, Warren.   Posture and Gesture. London,
    Duckworth, 1965.

Lamb, Warren and Turner, David.   Management
    Behavior. New York, International
    Universities Press, 1969.

Preston-Dunlop, Valerie. Handbook for
    Modern Educational Dance. London,
    Macdonald and Evans, 1963.